MW00595734
To: Gammy.
From: Mason & Maya

Grandmothers

are the best

Published by Sellers Publishing, Inc.

Sellers Publishing, Inc.
161 John Roberts Road, South Portland, Maine 04106
Visit our Web site: www.sellerspublishing.com • E-mail: rsp@rsvp.com

Mary L. Baldwin, Managing Editor
Charlotte Cromwell, Production Editor
Compiled by Charlotte Cromwell
Cover & interior design by Charlotte Cromwell

Cover & interior image credits © 2018 Floral Deco/Shutterstock.com; with the following exceptions pp. 6-7, 8, 16, 21, 30-31, 45, 51, 63 © 2018 Flaffy/Shutterstock.com; pp. 24-25 © 2018 Moshbidon/Shutterstock.com; pp. 42-43 © 2018 Chamille White/Shutterstock.com.

ISBN 13: 978-1-4162-4640-4

10 9 8 7 6 5 4 3 2 1

Printed in China.

Grandmothers

are the best

It's such a grand thing to
be a mother of a mother –
that's why the world
calls her grandmother.

If I had known how
wonderful it would be
to have grandchildren,
I'd have had them first.

A house needs
a grandma in it.

A grandma is warm hugs and sweet memories. She remembers all of your accomplishments and forgets all of your mistakes.

Grandmothers hold their grandchildren in a special place in their heart.

There's no
place like home
except Grandma's.

Grandmothers
are wonderful
ladies who always
seem to place others
in front of themselves.

A grandmother is a little bit parent, a little bit teacher, and a little bit best friend.

Grandmother –
a wonderful mother
with lots of practice.

If nothing is going well,
call your grandmother.

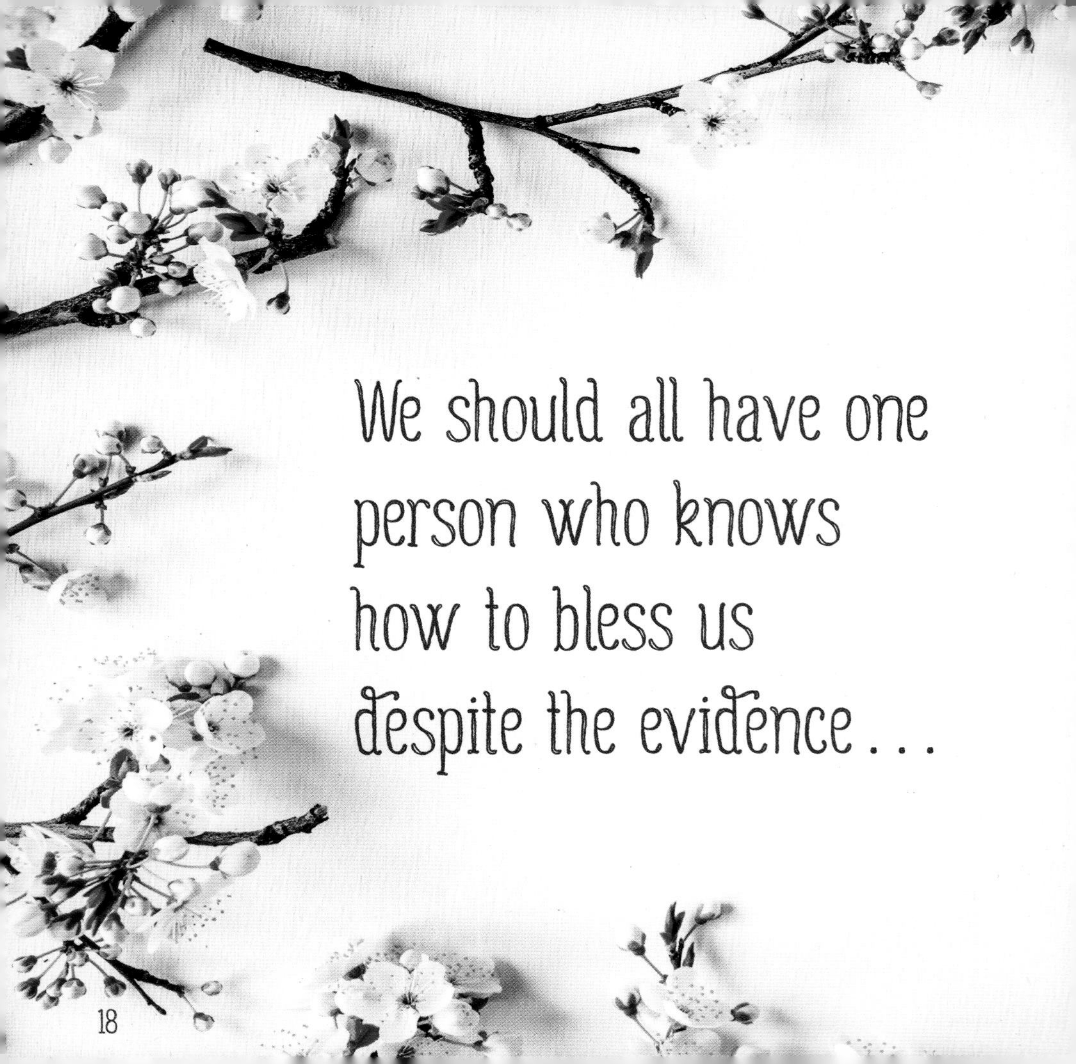

We should all have one person who knows how to bless us despite the evidence . . .

Grandmother was
that person to me.

You do not really
understand something
unless you can
explain it to your
grandmother.

A garden of love grows
in a grandmother's heart.

When a child is born,
so are grandmothers.

Becoming
a grandmother
is wonderful.

One moment you're just a mother. The next you are all-wise and prehistoric.

Grandma always made you feel she had been waiting to see just you all day and now the day was complete.

Grandmas
never run out
of hugs
or cookies.

Perfect love sometimes does not come until the first grandchild.

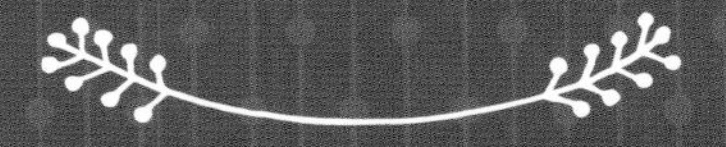

Grandmas hold our
tiny hands for just
a little while . . .

. . . but our hearts forever.

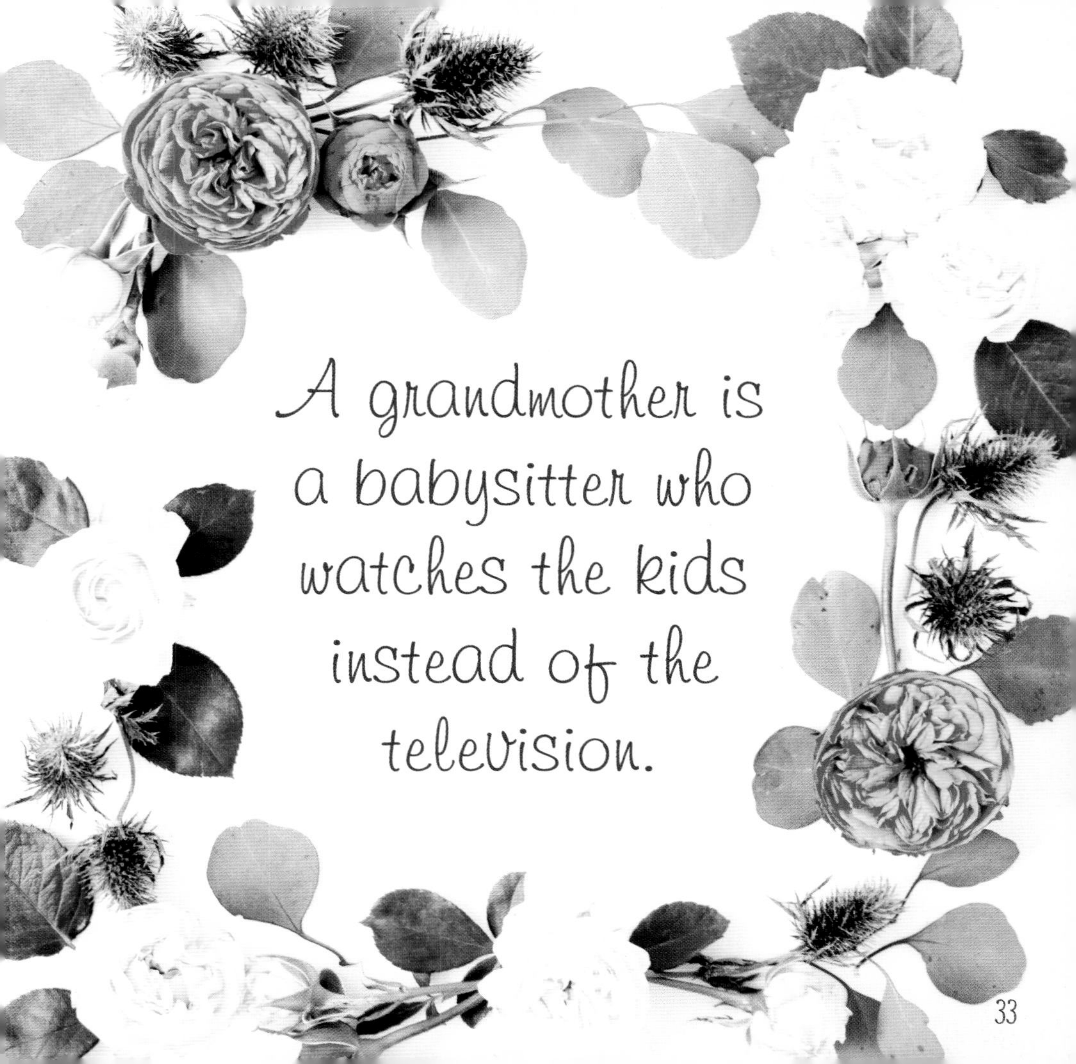

A grandmother is
a babysitter who
watches the kids
instead of the
television.

It is as grandmothers
that our mothers come
into the fullness
of their grace.

A grandmother is
a safe haven.

Nobody can do for little children what grandparents do.

Grandparents sort of sprinkle stardust over the lives of little children.

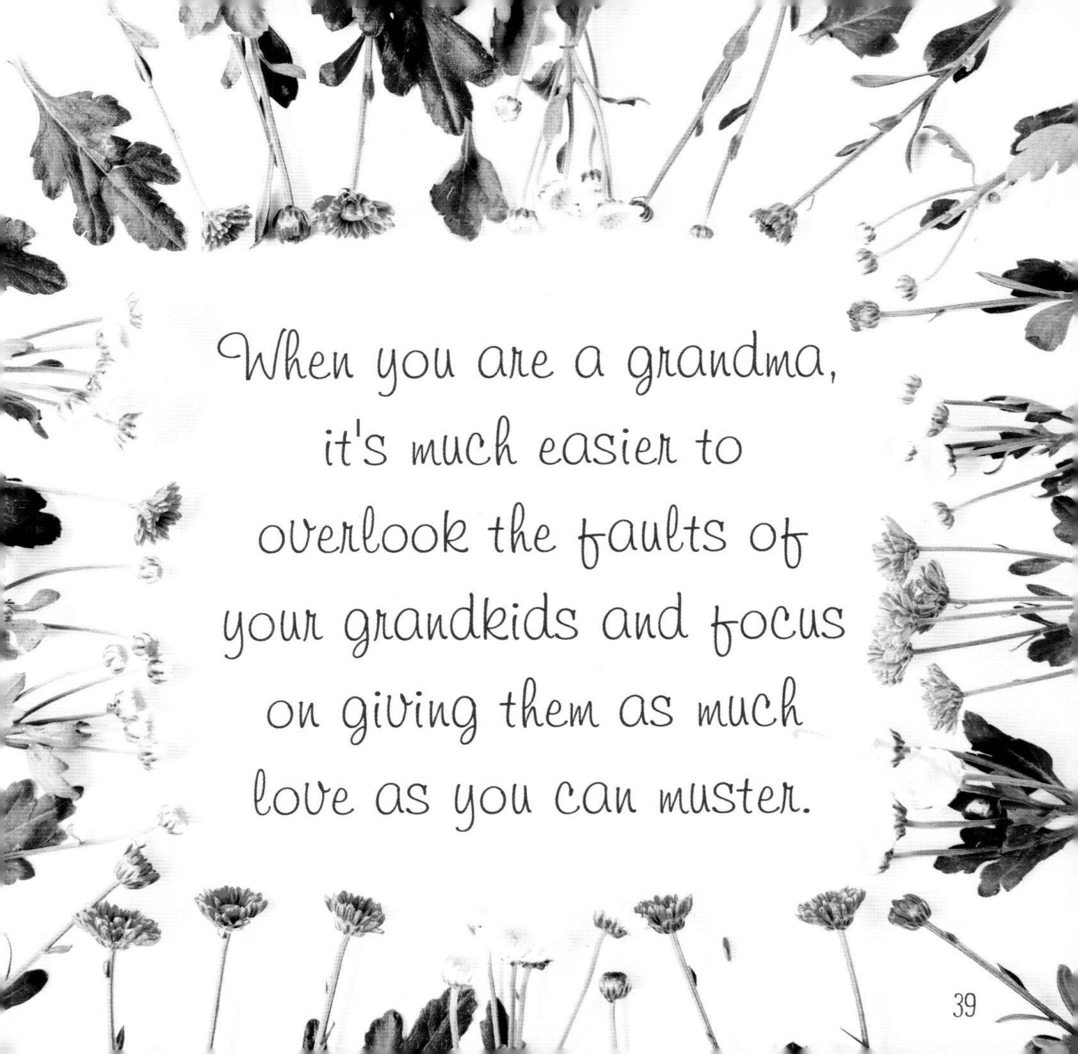
When you are a grandma,
it's much easier to
overlook the faults of
your grandkids and focus
on giving them as much
love as you can muster.

Grandmothers always
have time to talk and
make you feel special.

Grandmas are moms
with lots of frosting.

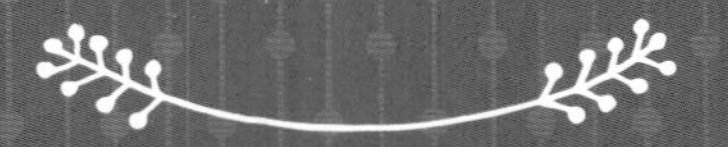

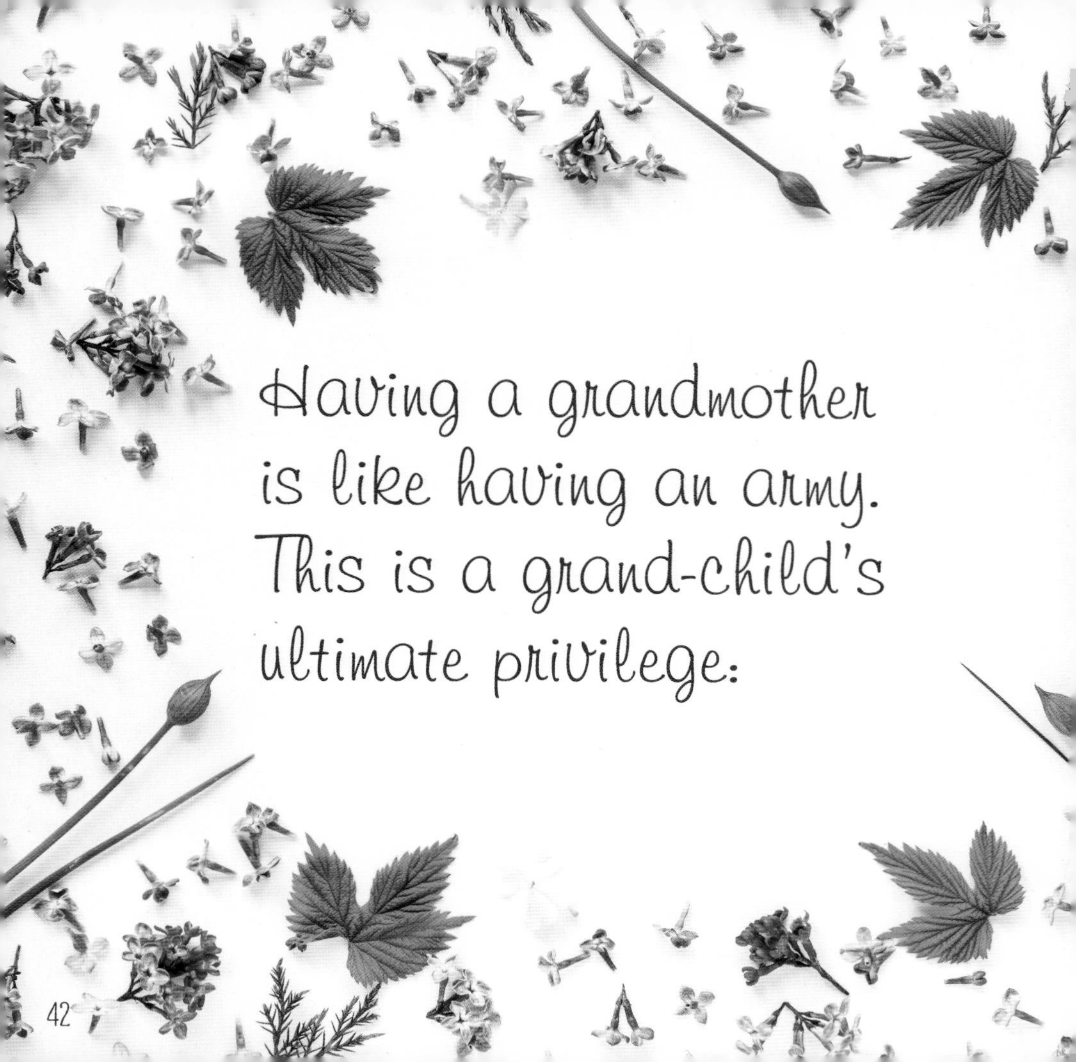

Having a grandmother
is like having an army.
This is a grand-child's
ultimate privilege:

knowing that someone
is on your side,
always, whatever
the details.

Grandma serves kisses, counsel, and cookies daily.

Grandmother-grandchild relationships are simple. Grandmas are short on criticism and long on love.

If your baby is "beautiful and perfect, never cries or fusses, sleeps on schedule and burps on demand, an angel all the time," you're the grandma.

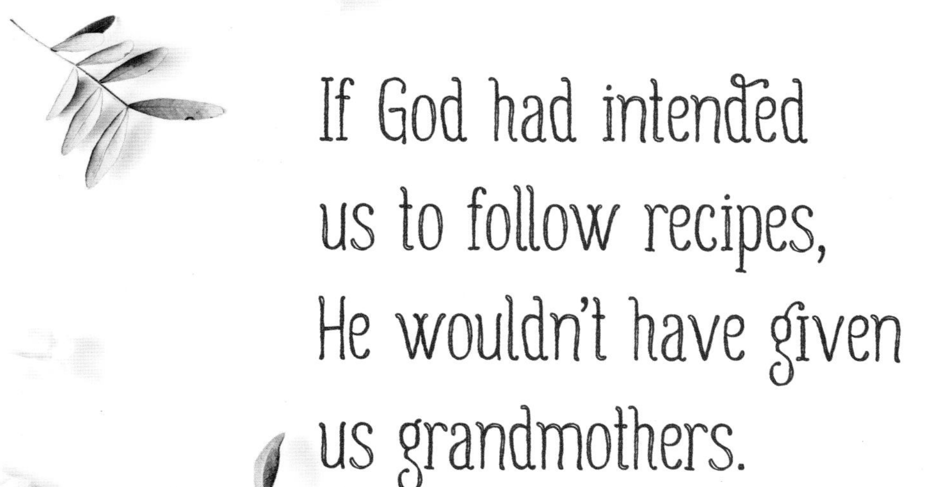

If God had intended
us to follow recipes,
He wouldn't have given
us grandmothers.

Unconditional
positive regard is rarely
given by anyone except
a grandmother.

Grandmothers sprinkle stardust
over children's lives.

Grandmothers are a
delightful blend of laughter,
caring deeds, wonderful
stories, and love.

A mother becomes a true grandmother the day she stops noticing the terrible things her

children do because
she is so enchanted
with the wonderful things
her grandchildren do.

When grandparents enter the door, discipline flies out the window.

A grandmother pretends she doesn't know who you are on Halloween.

I loved their home. Everything smelled older, worn but safe; the food aroma had baked itself into the furniture.

Just about the time a woman
thinks her work is done,
she becomes a grandmother.

You are the sun,
Grandma,
you are the sun
in my life.

Quote Credits:

p. 5 Author Unknown; p. 7 Lois Wyse; p. 8 Louisa May Alcott; p. 9 Barbara Cage; p. 10 Catherine Pulsifer; pp. 11, 13, 15, 16 Author Unknown; p. 17 Italian Proverb; pp. 18-19 Phyllis Theroux; p. 21 Proverb; p. 22 Author Unknown; p. 23 Judith Levy; pp. 24-25 Pam Brown; p. 27 Marcy DeMaree; p. 28 Author Unknown; p. 29 Welsh Proverb; pp. 30-31, 33 Author Unknown; p. 34 Christopher Morley; p. 35 Suzette Haden Elgin; pp. 36-37 Alex Haley; p. 39 Author Unknown; p. 40 Catherine Pulsifer; p. 41 Author Unknown; pp. 42-43 Fredrik Backman; p. 45 Author Unknown; p. 46 Author Unknown; p. 47 Teresa Bloomingdale; p. 48 Linda Henley; pp. 51, 52, 53 Author Unknown; pp. 54-55 Lois Wyse; p. 57 Ogden Nash; p. 58 Erma Bombeck; p. 59 Susan Strasberg; p. 60 Edward H. Dreschnack; p. 63 Kitty Tsui.